5805   82

A SHOT IN THE PARK

WILLIAM PLOMER

A Shot in the Park

Jonathan Cape

THIRTY BEDFORD SQUARE . LONDON

FIRST PUBLISHED 1955

00025943

C10150
PRINTED IN GREAT BRITAIN IN THE CITY OF OXFORD
AT THE ALDEN PRESS
BOUND BY A. W. BAIN & CO. LTD., LONDON

CONTENTS

The author makes grateful acknowledgments to the editors of the *Listener*, the *London Magazine*, *Encounter*, and *Courier*.

THE NAIAD OF OSTEND:
or, A Fatal Passion

[In vol. I, chap. XIV, of *What I Remember* (1887), by
Thomas Adolphus Trollope, the brother of the novelist,
there is an account of life at Ostend during the bathing
season of 1835. He records some of the gossip and
scandals and mentions some of the more conspicuous
characters – Captain Smithett, for example, who com-
manded a Channel boat called the *Arrow*, was dashing,
handsome, and an immense favourite with the smart set
at Ostend. Smithett showed him one day an anony-
mous billet-doux which he had received, together with
a latchkey. The letter had been written by the very
pretty wife of a Belgian banker, and began: '*O toi, qui
commandes la Flèche, tu peux aussi commander les
cœurs.*'

The season, says Trollope, was a very amusing one,
and he had found himself in what he calls 'a queer and
not very edifying society, exceedingly strange, and
somewhat bewildering to a young man fresh from
Oxford who was making his first acquaintance with
Continental ways and manners. All the married
couples seemed to be continually dancing the figure of
chassée-croisez.'

Into this evidently lively little world there came a
mother and daughter, and this is how Trollope
describes them:

'We made acquaintance at Paris with a Mrs Mackintosh and her daughter, very charming Scotch people. Mrs Mackintosh was a widow, and Margaret was her only child. She was an extremely handsome girl, nineteen years of age, and as magnificent a specimen of young womanhood as can be conceived. "More than common tall", she showed in her whole person the development of a Juno, enhanced by the vigour, elasticity and blooming health of a Diana. She and her mother came to Ostend for the bathing season. Margaret was a great swimmer; and her delight was to pass nearly the whole of these hot July days in the water. Twice, or even thrice, every day she would return to her favourite element. And soon she began to complain of lassitude, and to lose her appetite and the splendour of her complexion. Oh! it was the heat, which really only the constant stimulus of her bathe and swim could render tolerable. She was warned that excess in bathing, especially in salt water, may sometimes be as dangerous as any other excess, but the young naiad, who had never in her life needed to pay heed to any medical word or warning, would not believe, or would not heed. And before the September was over we followed poor Margaret Mackintosh to the little Ostend cemetery, killed by over-bathing as if she had held her head under water! This sad tragedy brought to a gloomy end a season which had been, if not a very profitable, a very amusing one.'

It is on this passage that the following ballad is chiefly based.]

1. THE ARRIVAL

Ostend, eighteen thirty-five –
　Don't you know the reason
For the crowds along the front?
　It's the bathing season!

Kursaal windows flashing bright,
　Bands and fountains busy,
Pigeon-shooting, valsing, loo –
　Enough to turn you dizzy.

Such a press of elegance,
　Fribbles, belles and smarties,
Feathered heads and painted fans,
　Balls and picnic parties.

Such a flash of carriage-wheels,
　Seas of light to swim in,
Sparkling water, sparkling wine,
　Sparkling eyes of women.

Nightly, nightly now the moon
　Lights the dreaming ocean,
And at noon towards it flows
　The muslin tide of fashion.

Into this amusing world
　By the dancing-water
Enter Mrs Mackintosh
　And Margaret, her daughter.

Fresh from Paris, full of charm,
 The widow sports a bonnet
Envied for the tartan bows
 And ears of corn upon it.

Margaret is just nineteen,
 Tall as any goddess –
Dian in that springy step,
 Juno in that bodice.

Belgians marvel at her bloom,
 Flâneurs at her figure –
Highland mists for rosy cheeks,
 Breakfast oats for vigour.

'Mother, mother, may I bathe?'
 'Yes, my darling daughter!
See the gaily striped machines
 Drawn up to the water.'

'Mother, mother, may I bathe?'
 '*Again*, my darling daughter?'
'Ostend is so very hot,
 It's heaven in the water.'

'Mother, mother, may I bathe?'
 'Meg, my darling daughter,
I can't think where you get it from,
 This passion for the water.'

2. THE COMMENT

'Your daughter seems to adore
　　Above all things the sea —
She *shuns* the land, Madame.'
　　'Monsieur, you're telling me!

Three times a day she bathes,
　　She finds Ostend so hot.'
'Madame, a dip is good;
　　Excess, I fear, is not.'

'Indeed, I sometimes fear
　　Some secret strange allure,
And yet I know the sea
　　Is above all things pure;

The sea's her element,
　　She loves to feel aloof.'
'Ah, but a Mackintosh
　　Should be more waterproof.'

3. SOCIAL EVENINGS

Fashionables delight in
　　Evenings at the Fauches',
Pleasant English visitors
　　Attentive on the couches;

Madame B., in yellow silk,
   Fingering the spinet,
Mary Fauche, the Consul's wife,
   Singing like a linnet.

Here and there an *œillade*,
   A look of *carpe diem* –
'Taste these sweets, they're tempting,
   Just to please me, try 'em!'

Ripe and burning August moon
   Over midnight ocean –
Neptune's manly bosom heaves
   With a deep emotion.

'Mother, mother, may I swim?'
   'What, *at night*, my daughter?
The bathing-women have gone home,
   There's *no one* in the water!'

Now the nights are dry and warm,
   And the moon grows bigger,
All the married couples dance
   The chassée-croisez figure.

Madame L., the banker's wife,
   Writes to Captain Smithett,
Sending him a billet-doux
   And a latchkey with it –

'*Toi qui commandes la Flèche*
  Peux commander les cœurs – '
History will not relate
  How he answers her.

Colonel Dickson likes to give
  Dinner parties often;
When he looks at Margaret
  His martial features soften.

Baron Melfort makes himself
  Sweet as sugar candy,
But she never turns a glance
  On that randy dandy.

Margaret turns her head away,
  Feeling bored and pestered,
Turns her lovely sea-green eyes
  Outward, seaward, westward.

4. THE REPROACH

'Margaret, I wish to find
  A husband for my daughter,
But ever since we came you seem
  Quite wedded to the water.

The Baron with his quizzing-glass
  And wealthy Colonel Dickson
Must think you not a naiad but
  Some kind of water-vixen;

Each is looking for a wife,
  But neither man has got a
Wish to join his fortunes with
  A two-legged female otter.

Come out, my girl, and dry yourself,
  And let them see your figure,
Come out before your skin gets burnt
  As black as any nigger!'

'Mother, mother, I must bathe!
  Your own unruly daughter
Has found the truest, truest bliss
  Awaits her in the water.'

5. ECSTASY

Neptune loves the breast-stroke
  As Margaret loves the sea,
And now it is his best joke
  To keep her from her tea;

While mother bakes in dudgeon
  Beneath the hot sea-wall,
And sees her do the trudgen,
  And sees her do the crawl,

Neptune smoothes each contour,
  Each long elastic leg,
With not a soul *à l'entour*
  Embraces blooming Meg;

As supple as a porpoise
  She welcomes his advances –
Ah, Neptune, *habeas corpus*!
  The gods have all the chances.

6. THE DECLINE

August grows older,
  Thunder in the air,
The pace grows slower
  In this gay Ostend,
And tarnished summer
  Seems to declare
That light abandon
  Meets a heavy end.

Parasols are folded,
  Awnings fade,
Fans still flutter
  In the afternoon shade,
They're eating ices
  In the Royal Arcade,
Soon it will be time for
  Bills to be paid.

'*Madame! et comment*
  Se porte-t-elle
Meess Marguerite?
  D'une taille si belle!'

'Thank you, she's not
    Herself, I'm afraid –
Even upon her
    This heat must tell;

She has eaten nothing
    Since Saturday night,
And seems so languid –
    It can't be right –
I'm quite alarmed –
    Uncommon pallor –
I do protest she
    Looks quite yaller.'

7. THE END

'Mother, mother, one more bathe!'
    'Is it wise, my daughter?
I vow you owe this lassitude
    To long hours in the water.

That is what the doctor thinks;
    Now wouldn't it be wiser
To listen to the counsel of
    Your medical adviser?

You say the sea alone can cool
    This low and wasting fever,
But truly, truly Neptune is
    Like all men, a deceiver.'

Margaret gave her mother then
　A look that might appal,
And with a last low moan she turned
　Her face toward the wall –
　　And that was all.

8. THE EPITAPH

Here lies the Naiad of Ostend
　Who swam to an untimely end,
But now with her the Cherubim
　Delight in Seas of Grace to swim;
O happy Mackintosh, to share
　That everlasting *bain de mer*!

A RIGHT-OF-WAY, 1865

[An old bass-viol was lately bought for a few shillings at a farm sale not a thousand miles from Mellstock. Pasted on the inside of it was the following poem in a well-known handwriting. It is regretted that technical difficulties prevent its reproduction in facsimile.]

Decades behind me
When courting took more time,
In Tuphampton ewe-leaze I mind me
Two trudging aforetime:
A botanist he, in quest of a sought-after fleabane,
Wheedling his leman with 'Do you love *me*, Jane?'

Yestreen with bowed back
(To hike now is irksome),
Hydroptic and sagging the cloud-wrack,
I spied in the murk some
Wayfarer myopic Linnaeus-wise quizzing the quitches
And snooping at simples and worts in the ditches.

Remarked he, 'A path here
I seek to discover,
A right-of-way bang through this garth here,
Where elsewhiles a lover
I prinked with a pocket herbarium, necked I and
cuddled:
Now I'm all mud-besprent, bored and be-puddled.

I'm long past my noon-time.
The Unweeting Planner
Again proffers bale for one's boon-time
By tossing a spanner
Or crowbar into the works without recking the cost, sir.
At eighty,' intoned he, 'life is a frost, sir.

When erst here I tarried
I knew not my steady
Had coolly, concurrently married
Three husbands already,
Nor learnt I till later, what's more, that all three were
brothers,
Though sprang they, it seems, of disparate mothers.

Well, we two inspected
The flora of Wessex;
More specimens had we collected
Had she pondered less sex;
We botanized little that year ... But I must be
wending;
My analyst hints at amnesia impending.'

THE BUNGALOWS

In lofty light the towers dissolve
Of yellow elms this tranquil day,
Crumble in leisurely showers of gold
All Turneresque in bright decay.

The elms disperse their leaves upon
A nineteen-thirty builder's row
Of speculative dwellings, each
An unassuming bungalow.

Like concave shells, or shades, or shields
That guard some life or light aloof,
Like hands that cup a flame, or keep
Some frail and captured thing, each roof.

If high-pitched hopes have gone to roost
Where low-pitched roofs so smoothly slope
Perhaps these autumn rays diffuse
A deeper anodyne than hope.

Between the vast insanities
That men so cleverly invent
It may be here, it may be here,
A simulacrum of content.

Though separate only from the road
By five-foot hedge and ten-foot lawn
Each semi-isolationist
Seems almost from the world withdrawn,

Except that from a roof or two
Those thin and wand-like aerials rise
That suck like opium from the air
Bemusement for the ears and eyes.

The denizens of each hermitage,
Of 'Nellibert' and 'Mirzapore',
Bird-watchers all, in love with dogs,
Are primed with useful garden-lore:

Cabbage the emblem of their life –
Yet mauve the michaelmas-daisy glows
And under reddening apples gleams
A pearly, pure, belated rose.

Begrudging vulgar fantasy
To cheap and ordinary homes,
Discrimination might deplore
That concrete frog, those whimsy gnomes,

Nor see them as blind tribute to
The rule of dreams, or as a last
Concession to the irrational,
The old, wild, superstitious past.

The commonplace needs no defence,
Dullness is in the critic's eyes,
Without a licence life evolves
From some dim phase its own surprise:

Under these yellow-twinkling elms,
Behind these hedges trimly shorn,
As in a stable once, so here
It may be born, it may be born.

A SHOT IN THE PARK

*[Based upon an incident in the memoirs of the
Edwardian hostess, Mrs Hwfa Williams.]*

1

In the light beneath the leafage
In the afternoon in May
In the Park and near the Row
Gracefully from Hwfa[1]
Mrs Hwfa Williams turned away,
Saying 'Hwfa, I must go,
I expect a mob for tea;
Such fun, but I must fly —
You dine, I think, with me?
Till then, my dear, good-bye!'

Mrs Hwfa Williams
Twirled and furled her parasol,
Lightly stepped into her carriage,
Thinking it was all such fun —
Life, and May, and marriage.

Such a pretty moment —
How were they to figure
Fate in ambush, taking aim,
Finger on the trigger?

Later in a tea-gown talking
Over twinkling tea-things on a tray
(Hwfa in the Park still walking)
She was heard to say:

[1] Pronounce *Hoofer*.

27

'When my husband and I gave it out
We should move to Great Cumberland Place
My sister-in-law gave a shriek –
"My dears, you'll be lost without trace!"
    And she said it with such a grimace!

"It's so utterly out of the world!
So fearfully wide of the mark!
A Robinson Crusoe existence will pall
On that unexplored side of the Park –
    Not a soul will be likely to call!"

Disparaging all one adores,
Relations are such a disgrace;
They gossip, as bluebottles buzz,
They deplore what one is and one does –
    But they call at Great Cumberland Place!'

2

At home the tea-time tittle-tattle; in the Mall
Two different orbits about to intersect:
That a poor clerk and Mr Hwfa Williams
Should there converge nobody could expect
And only a clairvoyant could foretell.

Gravely conferring with a crony, Hwfa
On one side saunters; on the other glares
A young man, seemingly a loafer,
Whose small brain, infinitely busier than theirs,
Has been inflamed by Post Office affairs.

He sends the telegrams that other people write;
From overwork a breakdown now impends;
Abrupt, elliptic phrases day and night he sends,
Recurring in his fevered brain all day
To be reiterated in his brain all night.

Now all's confused, things are not what they seem,
He stands bemused, as if he had been drinking;
Life is a cryptic, an intolerable dream –
RETURN TONIGHT AUNT HENRIETTA SINKING:
CONGRATULATIONS DEAR FROM ALL AT CHEAM.

GLOXINIA WILTING ORDER PINK GERANIUM:
TEN THOUSAND OFFERED SILLY NOT TO SELL:
Telegraphese tattoos upon his eardrums,
Like red-hot tintacks drives into his cranium
The public syntax of his private hell –

THANK YOU BOTH ENCHANTED:
OIL CONCESSION GRANTED:
HOPE ARRIVE NUNEATON TEN TO EIGHT:
ARRIVING SEVEN MABEL STOP:
DON'T SELL REFECTORY TABLE STOP:
CAT OUT OF BAG YOUR TELEGRAM TOO LATE.

Suddenly he sees two frock-coats passing,
Two top-hats tilted in a tête-à-tête –
These are to blame! Revenge upon the senders
Of countless telegrams! He feels the uprush
Of a delayed explosive charge of hate.

He draws and points a pistol, then he shoots.
'Ouch!' cries Hwfa. Something has distressed him.
He stumbles, mutters 'Somebody has shot me!'
He falls. Blood falls upon his patent-leather boots,
And cries go up, 'A murderer! Arrest him!'

3

In the light beneath the leafage
Late that afternoon in May,
In the Mall and on the ground
Mr Hwfa Williams lay,
Happily not dead, but wounded.

'How do you feel?' they asked.
'Injured,' he said, 'and quite astounded.'

Mr Hwfa Williams
Was attended by a Dr Fletcher,
And vexed, but bravely bland,
Was carried home upon a stretcher;
And
On Mr Hwfa Williams' forehead
Mrs Hwfa Williams laid a
Ministering angel's hand.

Later 'Hwfa', Mrs Hwfa Williams said,
'Do you prefer the sofa to your bed?'

'My dear, I don't mind *where* I lie;
What *does* it signify
When not a living soul can tell me why,
About to cross St. James's Park
I'm picked on like a sitting pheasant
By, so they tell me, a demented clerk,
A truant from the G.P.O., Mount Pleasant?
Too many wires, they say, had turned his brain –
But why he turned on *me* – no, *that* they can't
                                    explain.'

4

'Good morning, have you heard the news?
You'll be amazed!' 'Well, what?'
'I nearly fainted when I read
That Hwfa Williams has been shot.'

'My dear, your coffee's getting cold – '
'Well, does it matter in the least?'
All over London in the morning
Breakfast was a headline feast.

'Now here is what the paper says:
A dastardly assault . . . the crime
Seems without motive . . . an arrest was made . . .
Alleged . . . admitted . . . passing at the time . . .

A grudge . . . dispatch of telegrams . . .
Pistol discarded, lying in the mud . . .
Enquiries made at Mr Williams' home . . .
Life not in danger . . . shock and loss of blood.

No one is safe, it seems, these days:
To stroll across St. James's Park
Is to receive a bullet in the leg
From some unhinged, ferocious clerk:

A little learning, as our fathers knew,
Is certainly a dangerous thing;
The lower orders have been spoilt,
And now they mean to have their fling;

But though the world's all upside down
And England hastening to decay,
Ring for the carriage; we'll enquire
How Hwfa Williams is today.'

5

'Crikey!' said the butler, Crichton,
'Blocking up the blooming street
All these callers keep on calling –
No one thinks of my poor feet!

All the toffs with all their questions,
Leaving cards you can't refuse;
These reporters, nosy parkers,
Proper sharks they are for news.

I was not engaged to answer
Bells that jangle all the time,
These enquiries well might drive a
Better man than me to crime:

How's your master? Is he better?
Is his life in danger still?
Is it true a gang attacked him?
Do you think they shot to kill?

Can you tell us why they did it?
Anarchists? A Fenian plot?
More of this and I'll go barmy,
Like the lad that fired the shot.'

Carriage after carriage crowding,
Kind enquirers choke the street:
How is Mr Hwfa Williams?
'No one thinks of MY POOR FEET!'

6

'And so,' said Mrs Hwfa Williams,
Telling the story after years had passed,
'It seemed that half of London came to call.
Fruit, game and flowers came crowding thick and
fast,
Cards like confetti rained into the hall –
Such a great fuss, poor Hwfa was aghast
Yet pleased, I think, at such extreme concern,

c

More pleased than our old butler with it all –
Poor Crichton hardly knew which way to turn.

The street was jammed, the knocker and the bell
Clamoured together like two fiends in hell –
And where was Crichton? Nobody could tell!
At twelve o'clock my maid rushed in and said
"Oh, ma'am, he's drinking quarts of brandy neat –
Crichton's gone mad! I'll see to the front door!"
Not mad but drunk I found him. Bursting into song
With *Home Sweet Home*, he lurched and hit the
floor.
Abject when sober, Crichton said his feet
Had driven him off his head, nor had he known
That Hwfa's best old brandy was so strong . . .
Hwfa forgave him, he had been with us so long.

He stayed for years . . . Poor man, his race is run . . .
I also soon shall hear the sunset gun –
But in between times life has been *such fun*!'

ATHELING GRANGE:

or, The Apotheosis of Lotte Nussbaum

[*From a Sussex newspaper, October,* 1953:

'HOUSEKEEPER MISSING – Miss Lotte Nussbaum (48), who came to this country as a refugee from Nazi Germany before the war, is reported missing from Spindrift, Hydrangea-avenue, Atheling-on-Sea, where she has for some years resided as housekeeper to Mrs Elvaston-Clunch.

As Miss Nussbaum's shopping-basket is also missing, it is thought that she may have gone out to gather blackberries or mushrooms, and may be suffering from loss of memory. Search parties have failed to find any trace of the missing woman.']

1

A heavy mist. A muffled sea.
A cloth of cobwebs veils the grass.
Upstairs alone the refugee
    Sees autumn in her glass:

A touch of autumn in the air,
The knife of autumn in the heart
Of one too constantly aware
    Of living half apart.

Is comfort peace? Can it restore
The severed root within the mind?
Domestic service evermore
   Is not what hope designed:

Kindly and rich and not a fool
The widow whom she housekeeps for,
But unadventurous, so cool,
   So English, such a bore.

Today the harmless Mrs Clunch
Went up to London on her own,
And Lotte, dreamy after lunch,
   Feels even more alone:

She has no one to whom to turn
And reminisce of those lost lives
The autumn smell of leaf and fern
   So poignantly revives;

It quickens an old appetite,
This dank and thrilling smell;
She feels a craving now to bite
   Mushroom or Chanterelle;

Off with a basket she will go
To find if, where the fields begin,
Some palatable fungi grow,
   And if so, bring them in;

She knows the very ones to look for –
Fresh, firm, not too mature –
There'll only be herself to cook for,
    A secret epicure!

2

Lotte acquired upon her native hills
  The caution of a fungivore,
Knew how to look a *Giftpilz* in the gills
And where for *Steinpilz* one had best explore,
So now with confidence she reconnoitres,
Steps forward, backward, stoops, intently loiters.

Though no mycophagist could be more eager,
    She finds she isn't doing well,
After an hour her harvesting is meagre –
Two Puffballs, and a not too fresh Morel;
But strolling on beyond her usual range
She comes to the deserted Atheling Grange.

3

Where formerly curlews were calling
And orchises fell with the hay
The last of the meadows are falling
To bungalows gnawing their way;

The seaboard is doubly eroded –
To seaward by gale-driven water,
And inland, where fields are outmoded,
By inroads of bricks and of mortar;

But still, though its owners have died out,
An island of ilex encloses
A nineteenth-century hide-out
Once lovely with lawns and with roses;

The owls, who succeeded its owners,
Would quit it with screeches tonight
If they knew that the place is now known as
A 'ripe-for-development' site.

The state of the place is appalling –
What is wrongly described as a shambles;
Everywhere ivy is crawling
And striving to strangle the brambles;

Everywhere brambles are clinging
And creepers are climbing and creeping,
The nettles are ready for stinging,
The willows have reason for weeping;

The woods were cut down in the 'twenties,
The farm was sold off at a loss,
The lodge is kept only by woodlice,
The gateposts are padded with moss;

Bindweed has smothered the greenhouse,
The summer-house under the yew
Is now just a cannot-be-seen house
That commands an invisible view.

O house once delightfully lived in,
O Atheling Grange, did they build you
For dry rot and wet rot to feed on,
A medium for mould and for mildew?

Why ask such an imbecile question?
That rhetorical style has gone by,
And nothing would be more surprising
Than to hear the old ruin reply.

With bunches of bats on the ceilings
And droppings of rats in the hall,
The decline of the Grange is complete and
At any time now it may fall.

4

Though Lotte is aware how torn her coat is,
   Full steam ahead she ploughs and pushes
Tank-like through snags and tangled thorny bushes,
Quite undeterred by wire or warning notice,
Convinced this *Hintergarten* she has found
Will prove to be her happy hunting-ground.

How right she is – but God knows how she knew it!
   She's in a mycophil's Utopia
Where autumn, from a golden cornucopia,
Has tipped out every sort of Cèpe and Blewit.
She fills her basket quickly. New to her
Truffles one doesn't have to disinter;

Not new to her, but never yet so keen,
   So *appetitlich* and so rich
That mushroom smell; nor has she ever seen
The Beefsteak Fungus growing in a ditch;
Here on a stump some tender Buff Caps quiver,
There Pluteus swells, like Strasburg goose's liver;

And peering downward through a rusty grating
   Into what used to be the cellars
She sees there, prettily proliferating,
A multitude of little beige umbrellas,
Throngs of a choice and edible Boletus
That seem to say 'Come down, my dear, and eat us!'

'*Embarras de richesse!*' she might exclaim,
   If she could coin so French a phrase –
So many kinds she doesn't know by name,
All ready to be cooked in different ways:
But who to feed? She yearns to summon up
Her long-lost kin to sit with her and sup.

'*Himmel!*' she sighs . . . And at that very word
   Celestial choirs inflate the breeze,
Die ganze Vogelschar gets busy in the trees,
And then a band – a German band – is heard
Playing a waltz by Waldteufel or Strauss,
And all the lights light up inside the house.

'*Himmel!*' she cries. And so it is – she's right!
   Across the new-mown lawn advance
Her long-lost family, arrayed in white,
Her parents leading in a lively dance
Her brother, sisters, nieces, uncles, aunts,
With crowns and harps – a most unearthly sight!

Oh, what a welcome for Miss Nussbaum! See,
   All's *himmelhoch* and *himmelblau*!
Heaven is hers, and she is Heaven's now!
She's disembodied, disencumbered, free!
Lotte is free! . . . Tomorrow Mrs Clunch
Will have no drudge to cook her blasted lunch.

THE PALMER TRIPLETS

['At an old house near the Decoy, now converted into cottages . . . lived, in the reign of Henry VIII, Lady Palmer, the famous mother of the Palmer triplets, who were distinguished from other triplets, not only by being born each on a successive Sunday but by receiving each the honour of knighthood. The curious circumstances of their birth seem to be well attested.'
E. V. Lucas: *Highways and Byways in Sussex.*]

1. NINETEENTH CENTURY

Smoke from a chimney lazed
  (Seen in an old vignette);
'Dream and remember', wrote the smoke,
  'Or waken and forget';

Jotted against a cloud
  A spray of v-shaped birds
Spelt in their static formation-flight
  A message without words;

Summer was in the cloud
  And the heavy cumulus trees,
The drum of the sun-warmed ear was lulled
  By undertones of bees;

A crone with a load of wood
  Resting beside the road
Drugged with the obsolete afternoon
  Dozed by the old abode;

The stump of the courtly house
　Stood firm, the hag was bent
In a courtesy to approaching death,
　A bow that was permanent:

Peace like a coma shut
　The scene, that house, her bow,
From the great fine worrying world
　(As raging then as now);

Peace in the dormant house –
　Ah, but a puzzling thing,
The caption in Gothic script beneath
　Said 𝔑𝔢𝔴 𝔓𝔩𝔞𝔠𝔢, 𝔄𝔱𝔥𝔢𝔩𝔦𝔫𝔤.

How was it ever new
　This place imbued with age
An age before that view was drawn
　For an Early Victorian page?

2. SIXTEENTH CENTURY

For the long journey out of Kent new-dressed
In a white mantle with a fur-trimmed hood
Four hundred years ago at New Place stood
Sir Edward Palmer's bride; she stood stock-still,
Stared at the bold-emblazoned Palmer crest
And felt a strange surrender of the will.

Heraldic art in images proclaims
The worship of fertility and blood.
The Palmer totem, from the herald's stud,
Was half a panther, argent and irate,
And issuant from its eager head were flames
All proper, as from a domestic grate.

Alice, confronted with the panther, felt
Its teeth and flame-red breath and silver pelt
More than symbolic of her husband's race:
Its rampant beauty seemed to glorify
His new-found image in her inward eye,
Their love's ferocious joy and feral grace.

New Place, new wife, new Lady Palmer: married,
She found a promise in that gonfalon
And in the palm-branch that the panther carried –
Promise of victory in life's long war,
Promise of life, with peace to follow on.
She turned, she smiled, her diffidence all gone.

Famous in history and obstetric lore
The Palmer triplets. On a Sunday one
Was born; after a week a second son:
They say a woman's work is never done –
In labour still, Sir Edward's lady bore
On the third Sunday safely one son more.

'My loving pride has equally been shared
Between my sons', their ageing dam declared,

'My three bright panthers of a single litter –
Sir John, Sir Henry, and Sir Thomas Palmer,
Each son a champion and not one a quitter,
Each a stout stuffing for a suit of armour.

Henry the Eighth gave each the accolade
In turn for valour. My son John survives,
But two in earth, God rest their souls, are laid –
God rest them, they were valiant in their lives.
Henry died old in battle for this nation,
Tom was beheaded – for miscalculation.

My babes arrived without unseemly haste,
With health and strength all three by God were graced;
Myself like them must soon be laid in earth
But may be not forgotten in this land
(Old doddering dowager now with shaking hand)
Because of their unprecedented birth.'

3. TWENTIETH CENTURY

The stump of the aged house
   Remains exactly yet
As the graver saw it who set himself
   To devise a new vignette.

Passing the old decoy
   Look ahead through the thick
Upstart rods of elder and ash
   At the warm and rosy brick;

The chimney is still the same,
　Smoke rises, fire still warms,
But life takes on in the Tudor rooms
　New, un-Tudor forms;

Under the apple-trees
　Slacks hung up to dry
In a casual can-can slackly kick
　Towards the same old sky;

They seem to be keeping time
　To something on 'the Light':
The cowman's daughter's boy-friend goes
　With her to a dance tonight;

On the back of his motor-bike
　They're off to a Gala Hop,
She'll wear her apricot nylon dress,
　Her shoes from the Co-op.

Good luck to you, girl, with your new,
　Your healthy Sussex face,
And, boy, to you: and come back safe
　To this far from new New Place.

Though the panther-breed have moved
　To another sphere or shire,
A panther lurks in every heart –
　Beware, its breath is fire!

ANGLO-SWISS:
or, A Day among the Alps

['Stainless steel, automatic, antimagnetic, luminous, shockproof.' – *Advertisement of a Swiss watch.*]

1. THE WINTER GARDEN

A plot of shadow by the Berg Hotel:
  Beyond that pure cobalt
Dogs in the snow look larger,
  In snow snow-white like salt;

Firs on the ridge look taller,
  The glossy jackdaws fly
Above the plateau and the salt-pan snow
  Under a stainless sky,

And up, up, up, the superlative peaks
  Hone in a howling glare
Adamant blade-like edges
  Against abrasive air:

These are the Alps a brochure
  Explains are 'peerless viewed
From the Winter Garden of the Berg Hotel
  In all their altitude'.

Snug in the winter garden
  The obvious English wait,
Rendered voracious by the rarefied air
  They sit and salivate,

Gaze at the peaks upstanding
   Of Alps they need not climb,
The Frumpspitz, the Lockstock, the Kugelhorn,
   And keep an eye on the time;

One and all they look forward
   To much and frequent food,
And eupeptic fullness seems to foster
   A self-complacent mood;

'Alpine air may be bracing
   But let me tell you this,
Swiss-made watches are antimagnetic,
   And so, I find, are the Swiss.'

That's John, an Englishman, speaking;
   He thinks he's worldly-wise
And out of his wealth of inexperience
   Presumes to generalize:

'The Swiss,' he declares, 'are kindly,
   Diligent, clean, and free,
But no Swiss girl could ever wind up
   My heart's mainspring for me!

A race of congenital waiters,
   They rightly aim to please,
But the female Swiss has about as much glamour
   As a waxwork stuffed with cheese;

And I don't approve of neutrals –
 More cunning than the rest
Of us who have to fight for peace, they feather
 A purely selfish nest.'

'I don't agree,' said another,
 'I think you misjudge the Swiss,
You can search the world in vain for a people
 As well-behaved as this;

Avoiding perennial bloodshed,
 Unlike the unbalanced Powers,
They've achieved a standard of decent living
 I much prefer to ours:

How can you hold opinions
 So cheap, half-baked, untrue?
Have you ever stopped to think, I wonder,
 What the Swiss may think of you?'

2. THE SKI-LIFT

Hoisting expectant skiers
 Up from the valley below,
Up, up, up, a conveyor-belt travels
 Through snow-upholstered trees;
Bundles of raw material,
 Passively up they go
To be transformed to projectile shapes
 Launched on runaway skis;

D

The chair in front of him carries
    A figure John approves,
A pretty woman alone ascending
    To try the tempting slope;
As she turns her head to converse with him
    And the ski-lift smoothly moves,
Her voice and her face set moving
    The inward lift of hope:

'I hear you speak unkindly of the Swiss,'
    She says: 'Confess you do!'
(French, perhaps, from her accent?)
    'Perhaps,' he says, 'I'm wrong.'
'Oh, but have you ever stopped to consider
    What the Swiss may think of you?
How can you understand them?
    You haven't been here long!'

'I may be wrong,' he repeats it.
    'Oh yes, indeed you may,
So let me ask you to listen to a lecture
    I think it's time you heard:
Visiting England I noticed
    Only the other day
Things you forget when you try to make
    The Swiss appear absurd:

Travel on trains or buses,
    You can't see out for grime,
And even when you can your urban vistas

Make little or no appeal;
Read any English paper –
    A catalogue of crime!
Money is snatched by swarms of bandits,
    Even policemen steal;

Rash is the girl who ventures
    By unfrequented paths,
And likely to lose what is better kept
    Until she is decently wed;
Children are starved and tortured,
    And wives are drowned in baths,
Cupboards are crammed with strangled harlots
    Dragged by the hair from bed;

Some of your English women
    Invite an end so crude –
They dress so badly, and most perversely
    Cannot or will not cook;
Cigarette-smoking trollops,
    Ignorant, stupid, rude,
In dirty trousers and with painted nails
    How horrible they look!

Pipe in his mouth, and so complacent
    The Englishman is cold,
Far too often deserving
    His narrow, graceless wife;
Dead to the fears and longings
    That other hearts may hold,

His head is full of cricket and football,
  Not of the art of life:

Yours is a grasping, warlike race!
  I say with emphasis
Nobody loves the English –
  All right, I'm going to stop!
I've given a caricature of the English
  As you did of the Swiss –
Put it in your pipe and smoke it!
  But here we are – at the top!'

There at the top where skiers
  Confront the slopes in bliss
He can't help giving her sun-warm face
  A quick compulsive kiss:
'This very morning,' she teases, laughing,
  'You never dreamt of this!
My name is Yvette, and I must explain
  I happen to be Swiss!'

Away she flies and he follows,
  Their outthrust profiles glow,
Already their speed is fused with the frisson
  That expert skiers know;
Their hearts beat fast, beat faster,
  Where *she* leads he will go
With a sibilant, swift and sugary hiss
  Over the perfect snow.

3. THE SKATING-RINK

Luminous nights in the shockproof
  Alps are clear and dry,
Stars don't twinkle, they stare directly
  Out of a sterile sky;

Metabolistic rates are quickened, the tourists
  Sleep-drunk bedward go,
No one is out in the village –
  But lights light up the snow;

From the Berg Hotel the ice-rink
  Looks white, looks bright, looks false –
To an empty rink an amplifier
  Repeats the Skaters' Waltz;

The Skaters' Waltz continues
  Though never a skating pair
So late competes with the flying shadows
  Flung by the arc-lamp there;

Shadows of the wind-swung arc-lamp
  Scribble across the rink
And the light at once erases those frantic brush-strokes
  Dashed on the ice like ink.

For whom are the lights all burning,
  For whom is the music played?
Silence and darkness, any Swiss can tell you,
  Can't help the tourist trade.

Suddenly a pair of skaters
    Skim into startled sight,
Obeying the invisible conductor's baton
    Under the tolling light;

Fused in a wave-like rhythm
    They sway, a gathering wave,
And a dust of diamonds fumes and sprays
    From curves their skates engrave;

One figure is it, or two there?
    One shadow, black as jet,
Waltzing distorted, expanding and shrinking,
    Commingles John and Yvette.

BAMBOO:

A Ballad for Two Voices

1

SHE   However dry and windless
Cold days, hot nights may be,
Bamboo, incessant rustler,
Your restless leafage utters
A sound of wind and rain:
Nobody knows the nervous
Effect it has on me –
I cannot stand the strain,
Bamboo, I cannot stand it,
Your whispering campaign!

HE   I love, bamboo, your fidgets
And sudden sighs, bamboo;
Awake alone I listen
To secret susurration
Like paper scraping stone;
Stroking the inner surface
Of this old heart, bamboo,
Whisper to me alone
Your wordless reminiscence –
And resurrect my own!

SHE   Here is the explanation
Why what he loves I hate:
My husband was a sailor

Out on the China Station –
(If I had known him then!
It seems the best life offers
Is second-best, and late;
Unsure of *what* and *when*
A girl may miss her chances –
What did I know of men?)

The girl he'll never talk of
And never can forget
Has always come between us:
I see her sly and slant-eyed
Haunting some furtive wood,
Slender in silk, and artful;
The moment that they met
Her doubtful maidenhood
Pleased him beyond all reason –
She stole his heart for good.

Before I ever knew him
The dew, the down, the bloom
Were brushed away in Asia –
Hers was his startling April,
His wildfire blossoming.
The years of humdrum fondness,
The habit-forming room
Are quite another thing –
I hate her for devouring
His unrecurring spring!

HE   Her skin was like a primrose,
In sheets of silk her feet
Slender as sleeping finches
Slept while the snow was heaping
A feather barricade
Between us and the future:
At first, so sly and sweet,
It seemed an escapade,
But we were caught together –
Love caught us while we played.

I felt her small heart racing,
Quick heart imprisoned in
Her flexile, bird-boned body,
As if another being
Conscious that it was mute
Beat desperate, beat lonely,
Against the screen of skin:
The hot moon smelt of fruit,
Looming up huge to listen
To one thin bamboo flute.

And that is why I planted
A thicket of bamboo
Here in an English garden –
Waving bamboo was witness
Of all that love can be:
I live at home and listen,
And you revive, bamboo,
After a life at sea,

The only overwhelming
Love ever shown to me.

SHE

How I dislike the supple
Canes, and the harsh coarse leaves!
There's something so suburban
About bamboos.

HE

                    The waving
Bamboo recalls the sway
Of young and fertile bodies
And lifted, long, silk sleeves.

SHE

Suburban, as I say.

HE

The wordless reminiscence
Is whispered night and day.

2

SHE

Now that he's dead and buried
At last, at last I'm free
To make my chosen changes
Put off when he was living:
I'm captain now, and crew –
(No freedom like a widow's!) –
And who's to disagree
With what I mean to do?
Root, shoot, and stem and sucker,
I'll root out that bamboo!

HIS GHOST (*softly, from a distance*)
    That's what you think, old helpmate,
    But always I shall swim
    Along your psyche's courses,
    The frogman in your bloodstream
    You never can evade;
    By cutting down that sappy
    Bamboo you'd injure him
    Whose peace of mind you made –
    You know you'll never touch it
    With secateurs or spade!

3

HIS GHOST Bamboo, she used to hate you
    But lonely now she hears
    And half believes your voice is
    Not yours but mine – ironic
    That she discovers now
    A soft association,
    Even a source of tears,
    In what she once described as
    'A vicious rasping sound' –
    It now puts her in mind of
    Her husband underground.

SHE   Strange, that I used to hate you,
    His keepsake plant, bamboo!
    In solitude your sighings

Recall my old companion
And not his dreamt-of past.

HIS GHOST   We phantoms have our triumphs.

SHE   You're *my* plant now, bamboo!

HIS GHOST   She understands at last
Why I was pleased to hear you.

SHE   I understand at last.

HIS GHOST   Hush-hush those open secrets
You'll much rehearse alone
When we are both reduced to
Potential fertilizer
For plants like you, bamboo.

SHE   Two butterflies beside you
A moment on a stone –

HE   Would not be us, bamboo!
And now long life we wish you,
Long-loved, light-leaved bamboo.

HIS GHOST } *(together, very softly)*
SHE   Bamboo, bamboo, bamboo!